Writing as a Retail Business

Books for Writers' Series

By

S. D. Anderson, PhD

Writing as a Retail Business

S.D. Anderson PhD

> "There is something delicious about writing the first words of a story. You never quite know where they'll take you."
>
> — Beatrix Potter

Writing as a Retail Business

© 2020 by Sharon D. Anderson Ph.D.

This is a Creative Work of the author fixed in a tangible medium. All rights are reserved. In accordance with the U. S. Copyright Act of 1976 and the DMCA (Digital Millennium Copyright Act), the scanning, uploading and electronic sharing of any part of this book without the written permission of the author/publisher is unlawful piracy or theft of the author's intellectual property. If you would like to use material from this book (other than for review purposes), prior written permission must be obtained by contacting the author sdanderson.books@gmail.com. Thank you for your support of the author's rights.

©2015 by Sharon D. Anderson, Ph.D.

2nd Edition 2016

3rd edition 2017

Anderson, PhD, Sharon D.

Writing as a Retail Business

S.D. Anderson PhD

Writing as a Retail Business

Books for Writers' Series

Summary: How To Build A Successful Retail Business With Your Writing.

ISBN: 979-8647136626

Cape Cod Publishing

Cape Cod, MA 02632

capecodpublishing@gmail.com

Published in the U.S.A.

Writing as a Retail Business

S.D. Anderson PhD

Writing as a Retail Business

Contents

FIRST SNAPSHOT 21

ABOUT RETAIL.. 25

SECOND SNAPSHOT.................................. 27

THIRD SNAPSHOT 30

BACK TO WRITING: 36

FOURTH SNAPSHOT 38

FIFTH SNAPSHOT....................................... 40

DEFINE INDIE AUTHOR.............................. 45

What is an independent author?................... 45

SIXTH SNAPSHOT 48

SELF-PUBLISHING vs TRADITIONAL PUBLISHING... 52

Exclusivity... 53

   A Sole Proprietor, Sole Proprietorship 64

   Limited Liability Company 64

Writing as a Retail Business

Cooperative 65

Corporation 66

EXPENSES 69

EMPLOYEES OR SUB-CONTRACTORS 71

A BUSINESS PLAN OUTLINE 73

YOUR IMPRINT 75

YOUR INVENTORY 77

SCALABLE CAREER 79

MARKETING 81

BLOG.. 82

PODCASTS.. 84

E-mail Lists 87

WEBSITES 90

SOCIAL MEDIA 93

ROYALTIES 95

A PLAN FOR EACH BOOK 97

THE HOOK... 106

Writing as a Retail Business

Written Word Media 117
Draft2Digital or D2D 119
RESOURCES 121

Writing as a Retail Business

Writing as a Retail Business

Introduction

Each book published, each manuscript written becomes the author's own inventory to offer for sale to the public, either through the traditional publishing route or the Indie self-publishing route. No matter which route you choose, it stills boils down, in professional terms, to a retail business. One manuscript or ten, this is the inventory in the Author's store.

Writing as a Retail Business is an overview, a guide, pointing the way to creating an actual business, small or huge, from your writing. I've kept the guide "short and sweet", planting seeds for the author to edit, much as a plot ready to manifest.

If you have one book or twenty, you have the basis for a small business. Here is where you can make the decision to go from a writer (meaning your writing is no longer a hobby) to

Writing as a Retail Business

an author/entrepreneur (getting serious, and using your writing as a legal business, with actual income to support your lifestyle). This is not an easy decision, especially for writers, because writers are artists. To make this decision, you, the writer/artist, has to switch your thinking from your left brain (creative) to your right (logical). (UGH!)

My struggle with this was lengthy until I read about Plato's Chariot, and understood the concept of balancing both realms.

I still struggle at times, because of that Mystic side of my life. I publish in both Visionary Fiction and Visionary Non-Fiction. It makes little difference which sides of the genre you work in, you're still an artist creating writing, (your creative brain.) What you do with that manuscript afterwards becomes the business (your logical side of the brain).

Writing as a Retail Business

This little guide, my podcasts, blogs and websites are all part of my marketing, my Imprint, which I touch on in a later section. It has been an exciting and fulfilling journey for me and something I would like to share with fellow writers. I watch many of you sit there with your finished or almost finished manuscripts and wonder "Where do I go from here?"

It is my hope that this guide will point the way; give you some insights, ideas and inspiration to help you capture the excitement of this new digital age. The possibilities are endless… and keep growing every day.

I can only share what I have discovered and learned over the years and offer those resources and ideas. The rest is up to you. You can try some of the techniques, and ideas and see if they work for you. Who knows? We may

Writing as a Retail Business

see your next manuscript on the New York Times Best Seller List! Hooray!

Happy Writing,

Dedication:

This guide is dedicated to my Dad.

He taught me all about being an Entrepreneur. .

Writing as a Retail Business

Writing as a Retail Business

The three parts to an indie authors life

1. **The writing (all about you)**
2. **Publishing (all about the book)**
3. **Marketing (all about the reader)**

Writing as a Retail Business

Writing as a Retail Business

Snapshots

Writing as a Retail Business

FIRST SNAPSHOT

Who I Am And How I Got Here.

Before I started writing, I was in retail. I worked in retail stores selling clothing, rugs, wherever I could get a job. I also worked in two women's consignment shops. Then I decided to sell real estate (not very successfully) but took all the training and did the listings. Eventually I ended up running a small real estate office here on the Cape. All during this time I was studying for my Bachelors, Masters and finally my Doctorate.

My career in serious writing started in 2000 when I wrote my doctoral thesis. A doctoral thesis is set up in a specific format. I bypassed all the rules and presented my thesis in the form of a bound book. (Audacious Author even then).

After that I worked full time and began writing part time. What I wrote then was terrible; please pardon the language (it sucked). I have since discovered that this is the norm for every aspiring writer. (Phew) I returned to writing church bulletins and doing copy for a small publication (I got paid for that) and confined my personal writing to after hours. I persevered.

Every self-help book I read on writing pointed to one thing. They all advised aspiring writers to *write about something you know*. Well, I knew about Angels because I talked with them all the time (yes, I did and still do.) so I wrote a book about them. At that time, books about Angels were not on any traditional publishers list. There wasn't even a category that the book would fit in. Were there any readers for this stuff? I was writing for a very small market. Not many people wanted to read books about Angels.

It is interesting to note here that I still continue to write to that small market.

Here is where I began to explore self-publishing.

Somehow I was led to BookLocker.com. Would they consider publishing a book about Angels? Yes, gladly. And that was the beginning of a long relationship with Angela and Richard Hoy and their publishing business. It was also the beginning of my relationship with their cover designer, Todd Engel of Engel Creative.

I published four print-on-demand (POD) books with them and just recently a fifth. I recommend then highly. Here is their link: www.booklocker.com

Writing as a Retail Business

In 2008, a young company (Amazon.com) was starting a new program for writers who wanted to publish their manuscripts. They had this new reader called a Kindle and needed stories for people to read on this electronic gadget. This was a DIY project (Do It Yourself). They offered free manuals and guides. That's when I became proficient with KDP (Kindle Direct Publishing) or publishing in e-book format. (The creation of that digital world). From there my books went flying onto KDP. I created a publishing entity: Angelic Communications which was my own publishing house. My books on KDP are published under this name. I now publish under Cape Cod Publishing, my new imprint and business.

I had never thought about using my books as a business, although I was probably getting to that point. I wanted my books to create enough additional income for me to eventually purchase a house or a place of my own where I could write. I wasn't completely clear on how to do that, I just knew that I could. At that point I discovered Joanna Penn of The Creative Penn. She is definitely someone to check out. I can only say good things about her. She has been a HUGE inspiration for me.

Here is her link: www.thecreativepenn.com

ABOUT RETAIL

Retail is retail no matter what product you are selling: Cosmetics (Mary Kay) yes, I even did that for a short time, Houses (Real Estate) told you about that, Clothing (Gap, August Max), crystals and stones (Little Shop of Crystals). Did I mention I had three of these shops at three different times and locations? One was in Vero Beach, Florida and two were here on the

Writing as a Retail Business

Cape. I recently closed the third crystal shop, and put the entire store inventory on-line.

As for my books, they are offered here on-line (E-Books, print books, Audio books). It's all inventory for sale to the public, and if you choose, a retail business.

SECOND SNAPSHOT

Who Are You And Where Are You Now?

Congratulations! You've written a book or perhaps several. The creative process is so exciting and gratifying. Getting words on a page, telling a story is a marvelous accomplishment. You should be proud. You finally made it from writer to author. Wave that book(s) as if it were show and tell and it is! You tell your friends and family, send them a copy. You market (tell your friends) your new accomplishment on social media, and sell a few copies in the local bookstores, do a few book signings, and wonder sometimes if that's all there is. This is how I treated my books, like crocheting scarves for Christmas gifts.

Writing as a Retail Business

During those preceding years, I downloaded and read countless books and ideas about marketing your books and playing the numbers on Amazon. None of that seemed too effective and very time consuming. I read books on selling by the big hitters; Dale Carnegie, Napoleon Hill, Tom Robbins, and *Rich Dad, Poor Dad* several times, did Masterminding, nothing seemed to click for me. I had 16 books on Amazon, some were selling, others, not. I also had another 5 books on my computer screen in process. I was 'off' somewhere, where was my focus? Then I discovered Joanna Penn and her site *The Creative Penn*. That's when everything changed for me. That's when my THINKING changed.

Retail had been part of my life for years, why not treat my books as inventory and use them to power a business. This process isn't always easy for everyone. Sometimes you have to

Writing as a Retail Business

THINK about it and (light bulb) hadn't I just finished writing a book titled: What Are You Thinking? Your Thoughts Create Your World. (Honestly!) Sometimes we need a coconut to fall on our heads. Was that a coconut or what?

THIRD SNAPSHOT

Where Are You In This Process?

Think about this for a moment. Where are you in this process with your books? Are you out there actively marketing those books from the trunk of your car? Are you still in the process of writing them and editing them again and again? (Procrastinating? I did that for months creating busy work under the pretext of 'writing') Are you waiting for one of the BIG FIVE publishing companies to come by your house and offer you a million dollar contract? OR are you sitting under a coconut tree crocheting scarves for Christmas? Tough questions but necessary.

I didn't want to look at what I was really creating. Then . . . . . I decided it was time to do something about this stable of books I had created with great intent and make them into a BUSINESS. Anyone who has ever had a retail business knows that you have to actively work at it, and it takes time and a plan. That's when I turned the corner and decided that I would create a real business using my books as inventory.

Are YOU ready to take your WRITING one step further? Are you ready to make it into A RETAIL BUSINESS?

Here is a little quiz for you that might help clarify where you are now and where you might want to be. These are easy questions and NO there won't be a quiz later. You can answer these questions easily.

Do you LOVE to write?

Does your writing give you satisfaction?

Do others like what you write?

Are your books selling?

Writing as a Retail Business

Do you wish you could sell more books?

Do you want your books to pay the bills?

Do you want your books to support you?

Do you have a lot more books you want to write?

Do you think your books could power a business?

Do you wish you had more time to write?

Do you believe your writing could become a full time career?

If you answered YES to some of these questions, are serious about your writing and think a *serious* career in writing is something you might want to consider, THEN READ ON.

Have you ever considered your writing as a business? I hadn't even thought of it. I already had a small business, a Little Shop of Crystals

Writing as a Retail Business

where I taught workshops. My writing was just a hobby. I wrote booklets for my classes, had a website, wrote a few books and published them on Amazon. Somehow, I wanted more. I also thought my writing was not very good.

So, I joined a weekly writers group in Osterville. (This step is highly recommended for any aspiring writer. Find a writers group to help you.). Here I worked on honing my skills (they certainly needed it), and learned a great deal about the craft of writing from other writers of like mind. After 3 years (Of being smashed and trashed by the group) I created another print book, a futuristic story centered on a crystal.

To this point, I had been using only digital formats for the last four years. Going back into print again was not something I was comfortable with. I had previously created four print books with BookLocker.com. Those books

Writing as a Retail Business

had NOT sold too many copies. So, I tried again to see if this time the market would be different. The lessons learned from this print book (again) and the process of book signings, etc. was very enlightening. I was in that same cycle again. I was in the proverbial 'rut'. This was NOT what I wanted to do with my writing, and the traditional publishing route was not my dream. I was far too independent, an Indie Author, an Audacious Author to the core.

As an aside, I am no longer in that group but have created several writing groups where my writers will never have to suffer the indignities that were delivered to me. Each member has become a friend and family to me. They are a unique bunch of exceptionally creative and loving writers. May you have the good fortune to find such a group!

Writing as a Retail Business

As an aside, many of the group's members are still holding that dream to traditional publish. I certainly wish them success and happiness.

BACK TO WRITING:

I wanted my books to sell because I felt they had a message for the reader. My intent was and is to inspire the reader. My 'slogan' is WEEI: Writing to Entertain, Educate and Inspire readers. I seriously wanted to earn more income from my books, but knew there had to be a better way, one I was not focusing on, another words, My focus was wrong. My THINKING was off. So, I started to educate myself again, this time with a focus of creating a business using my books as inventory. I downloaded more free books, workshops, podcasts, webinars, and purchased some audio books. I was inspired and re-focused. I have included these resources that I used and the links if you're interested at the end of the book.

Writing as a Retail Business

If you have those same feelings, then stay tuned. That's what this book is all about.

WARNING:

What this book **ISN'T** about is a get rich quick scheme, or how to work the Amazon system to sell more books. If you are truly interested in creating a retail business with your books it takes time, just like any business. The beauty of creating this type of business is that it will support you for years to come. Others refer to this as a 'Laptop Lifestyle' meaning you can take this business with you anywhere in the world.

THIS GUIDE IS ABOUT HOW TO BUILD A SUCCESSFUL RETAIL BUSINESS WITH YOUR WRITING.

FOURTH SNAPSHOT

What You Will Discover In This Guide

Self- Publishing vs Traditional Publishing

Determining Your Rights

One Manuscript – 6 Possibilities

Think Globally - The Digital Age

Small Business Options

Expenses

Employees or Sub-contractors

A Business Plan outline

Your Imprint

Your Inventory

A Scalable Career

Writing as a Retail Business

Marketing

Royalties

A Plan for Each Book

Resources – all in one place.

FIFTH SNAPSHOT

Who Are You?

DEFINE WRITER

*"A **writer** is a person who uses written words in various styles and techniques to communicate ideas. Writers produce various forms of literary art and creative writing such as novels, short stories, poetry, plays, screenplays, and essays as well as various utilitarian forms such as reports and news articles. Writers' texts are published across a range of media. Skilled writers who are able to use language to express ideas well often contribute significantly to the cultural content of a society. The word is also used elsewhere in the arts – such as songwriter – but as a standalone term, **"writer"***

Writing as a Retail Business

normally refers to the creation of written language. Some writers work from an [oral tradition](#)."

Source: Wikipedia

DEFINE AUTHOR:

*"An **author** is broadly defined as "the person who originated or gave existence to anything" and whose authorship determines responsibility for what was created. Narrowly defined, an **author** is the originator of any written work and can also be described as a writer."*

Source: Wikipedia

When you become an Author, which indicates you have written and published something or are in the process of doing so, then your writings can become <u>a profession or a career,</u>

if you so choose. When you define your writing as a business, your writing then becomes your profession or your career. !!

NOW, you can stay there and just be an author, rest on your laurels and play with those fifteen or twenty copies, wondering who you can give them to – OR - you can step over and become an AUTHOR/ENTREPENEUR. (Here is where the real fun begins!)

DEFINE ENTREPENEUR:

*"The **entrepreneur** is "a person who organizes and manages any enterprise, especially a business, usually with considerable initiative and risk." Rather than working as an employee, [an entrepreneur] runs a small business and assumes all the risk and reward of a given business venture, idea, or good or service offered for sale. The entrepreneur is commonly*

Writing as a Retail Business

seen as a business leader and <u>innovator</u> of new ideas and business processes."

(Don't you love that?)

"Entrepreneurs perceive new business opportunities and they often exhibit positive <u>biases</u> in their perception (i.e., a bias towards finding new possibilities and unmet market needs) and a pro-risk-taking attitude that makes them more likely to exploit the opportunity. Entrepreneurial spirit is characterized by innovation and risk-taking."

(Take a deep breath.)

"The exploitation of entrepreneurial opportunities may include actions such as developing a <u>business plan</u>, hiring the <u>human resources</u>, acquiring financial and other required resources, providing leadership and being responsible for the venture's success or failure. <u>Joseph Schumpeter</u> (1883–1950) stated that the role of the entrepreneur is

Writing as a Retail Business

"<u>creative destruction</u>" and the changes and "dynamic <u>disequilibrium</u> brought on by the innovating entrepreneur ... is the 'norm' of a healthy <u>economy</u>."

Source: Wikipedia

This is such a great description for a writer who is already a visionary (story line, plot, plan), an organizer (notes, ideas, characters), and a manager (of time and skills). The only thing missing here is the actual, physical 'business or enterprise'. That's the easy part. Read on.

DEFINE INDIE AUTHOR

What is an independent author?

At ALLi, "independent" is an inclusive description and always relative (everyone needs support to write and publish well). Some of our members are fiercely indie-spirited, as DIY as it's possible to be. Others are happy to collaborate with a publisher where that seems advantageous, some working with paid publishing services, others with trade publishers.

So what marks out an indie from other authors? The Alliance allows that you are an independent author if:

You have self-published at least one book.

Writing as a Retail Business

You see yourself as the creative director of your books, from conception to completion through publishing and beyond.

You expect that status as creative director to be acknowledged in any partnership you negotiate, whether a paid author-service, or in a deal with trade-publisher or agent e.g. if you have an established author platform, you should receive a higher royalty rate and advance than an author who does not.

You recognize that you are central to a revolutionary shift in publishing which needs to move from seeing the author purely as a resource (in the new parlance 'content provider') to respecting the author as a creative director, with much to offer — and be rewarded for — in each step of the publishing process.

You are proud of your indie status and carry that self-respect into all your ventures,

Writing as a Retail Business

negotiations, and collaborations for your own benefit and to benefit all writers.

Quote from ALLI The Alliance of Independent Authors.

http://www.allianceindependentauthors.org/ask-alli/

SIXTH SNAPSHOT –

Scalable Income

Each book you write is scalable income.

This term was a totally new concept for me. I had no idea what it meant. After researching it, I discovered that I really liked this idea. It fit so well with writing novels or books.

Scalable Income –

A scalable profession allows you to make more money without an equivalent increase in labor or time.

An Author writes a book one time and his effort is the same (basically) whether he or she sells 500 or 500,000 copies.

Source: Ben Casnocha

Writing as a Retail Business

http://casnocha.com/2009/03/scalable-vs-non-scalable-careers.html

Every author who writes a book is creating scalable income. He or she is creating what I call INVENTORY. The more inventory you create the more income. (Accounting 101) And you only have to do it once.

Example: "A" works at a computer for company "B". She makes $15.00 per hour. If she works 40 hours, she earns $600.00. To earn more money, she would have to work more than 40 hours. (Non-scalable income) See the difference?

Another scenario:

Your e-book is out offered on Amazon.com selling at $3.99 per copy. This book has a landing page and is offered in the U.S., the UK, Denmark, Italy, India, Canada, Brazil, France, Spain, Mexico, and Australia. (Hope I have all of the countries). You wrote this book once

Writing as a Retail Business

and here you have global scalable income. You can also offer your book on KOBO, or NOOK. You didn't have to write a book for each site. Scalable income – a scalable career.
.

Writing as a Retail Business

SELF-PUBLISHING vs TRADITIONAL PUBLISHING

If you have already published your book(s) with a traditional publisher, that's great! You can still create a business from this guide and make your business and your books a success. Most publishing houses today don't offer marketing services or do too much publicity as they used to in the past, unless you are a very established author with a large 'platform' (following) and books with tons of reviews. Another words, they want established authors in their 'stable'.

Self-published authors, on the other hand, are usually just beginning or have a few books to their credit. They know that their books won't sell unless they market them. OR they think that once their book is up on Amazon, it will sell itself. So sorry to have to tell you this, BUT, that book is not going to move unless you help it out. Marketing is a whole set of skills. I touch on this in another chapter.

<u>Basically, what we are talking about here is EXCLUSIVITY</u>

Exclusivity

With a traditional publisher, your manuscript belongs to your publisher exclusively. Another words, you don't own it anymore because your publisher bought your rights to that work. The duration would be listed in your contract. Some are for 3 years some are for more before you can have the rights to your work or manuscript.

Amazon offers exclusivity in their KDP contract. If you choose this benefit your work belongs to Amazon.com KDP for 90 days when you cannot sell your book anywhere else except on their sites. This option works fine for me because they do all the work and sell my book in thirteen different marketplaces: U.S., UK, Canada, Denmark, Netherlands, Spain, France, Japan, Brazil, Mexico, India, Italy and Australia.

When you self-publish, you can choose not to use the 90 day exclusive with Amazon and hold onto your rights then you are free to offer your book on their site, as well as KOBO, and NOOK. Those are the biggest ones. There are smaller sites that you can use also.

www.smashwords.com and www.draft2digital these two sites are what I call service sites. You send your book to them and they will shoot it out to additional market places. D2D sends them to www.scribed.com www.inktera.com and www.tolino.com as well as the original 4. I think of them as agents because they take 15% off the sales (profit) to use their services. You might consider that a savings if you don't want to deal with 8 different dashboards.

Another service you might consider for all aspects of publishing your manuscript is Fivver. Here is the link: https://www.fiverr.com/

For FREE BOOK SITES:

Free book sites are just that. You can offer your book on their sites for free for a limited time if you are doing a launch or free offer.

www.bookbub.com

www.freebooksy.com

www.bookgorilla.com

www.booksends,com

2. DETERMINING YOUR RIGHTS

"It's important to understand what rights you're selling or licensing away, not only to protect your interests, but to keep you out of legal hot water. Understanding rights can also help you make more money on a piece by -- legally -- reselling it again and again.

So, what are rights?

When you write something -- be it an article, short story, book, even a letter -- you automatically own copyright to that material. What you've written belongs to you. You don't have to fill out any forms or send away any registrations; the act of creation itself gives you copyright."

Source: http://www.writing-world.com/rights/rights.shtml

Writing as a Retail Business

If your books are published traditionally, you need to know what your rights are. Sometimes the publisher holds the rights to your work, and that is a limitation for those works, depending on the terms of your contract. If, however, you are self-published, or know for certain the rights belong to you. the possibilities and the opportunities are endless.

Recommendation: pull out your contract and see exactly what belongs to you. Note: Don't be disappointed if your publisher holds your rights to that piece.

Advice: Let that publisher hold those rights. Be generous because there are many more books where that one came from. As an author, you know that your supply of books and manuscripts is **unlimited!**

All you have to do is write them!!!

S.D. Anderson PhD

Writing as a Retail Business

3. ONE MANUSCRIPT – 9 POSSIBILITIES

From one manuscript here is what you can create:

Print book – hard or soft cover

POD book- (Print on demand)

E-Book – epub or mobi

E-Book with sound

Audio Book

A Series of books

A Novella

Serialize the book in magazines or publications

Your book published in another language.

From one book, you can create all of this scalable income, all of this inventory. Another aspect to writing is **an inexhaustible supply**! What writer has not experienced that next book as he is writing the current one? There is no limit to the inventory you can create.

4. THINK GLOBALLY – THE DIGITAL AGE

Let's face it; we are smack in the midst of a rapidly running current of technology. Almost everyone you know has a cell phone, right? Most of us have upgraded to a more sophisticated version, an iPhone, an iPad, or an Android. Most homes have a computer or a laptop, and internet. Children in kindergarten use computers and iPads and are most proficient on them. (These are all potential readers, by-the-way.)

Technology is moving rapidly and traditional publishing as we knew it has changed and is becoming less and less 'the writer's dream'. Indie Authors are the pioneers for the new publishing industry.

The Authors Earnings Report is published every quarter as they gather the information and report it. It is a great indicator of what is

Writing as a Retail Business

happening in the publishing world, and well worth a look.

Author Earnings Report September 2015

"These "non-traditionally-published" books now make up nearly 60% of all Kindle e-books purchased in the US, and take in 40% of all consumer dollars spent on those e-books.

Source:

http://authorearnings.com/report/september-2015-author-earnings-report/

These numbers have increased almost 65% over the past five years. Amazon has 4,102,338 e-books on Kindle to offer, (at this writing) most from Indie self-published authors, and the amount of audio books, 222,220 on Kindle (Audible is an Amazon Company) are growing. Amazon, Nook, iTunes, and Kobo now publish globally.

Writing as a Retail Business

On any day, I can click into my Amazon Author Account dashboard and see in what country, my books are selling, how many I have sold so far this month and I only publish in English. (More possibilities I vaguely mentioned before.) I am always amazed to see my books selling in Denmark or Australia. I could never have accomplished that with a traditional publisher, much less haul my copies around the world. I have the option of sitting in my house, in my pajamas writing and selling my books globally. Imagine that!

5. SMALL BUSINESS OPTIONS

*"**DEFINITION** of '**Business**' . An organization or enterprising entity engaged in commercial, industrial or professional activities. A **business** can be a for-profit entity, such as a publicly-traded corporation, or a non-profit organization engaged in **business** activities, such as an agricultural cooperative.*

Source: Business Definition | Investopedia

If you have decided to take your writing to creating an actual retail business then put on your business hat, crank up your left brain (or is it your right?) and let's talk about *business*.

You have the option here of creating a legal business and becoming a business owner. This has so many advantages. Here is the link for the Small Business Administration.

Writing as a Retail Business

https://www.sba.gov/category/navigation-structure/about-sba

Here are the main choices from their website.

A Sole Proprietor, Sole Proprietorship

A sole proprietorship is the simplest and most common structure chosen to start a business. It is an unincorporated business owned and run by one individual with no distinction between the business and you, the owner. You are entitled to all profits and are responsible for all your business's debts, losses and liabilities.

Source https://www.sba.gov/content/sole-proprietorship-0

Limited Liability Company

A limited liability company is a hybrid type of legal structure that provides the limited liability features of a corporation and the tax

S.D. Anderson PhD

efficiencies and operational flexibility of a partnership.

The "owners" of an LLC are referred to as "members." Depending on the state, the members can consist of a single individual (one owner), two or more individuals, corporations or other LLCs.

Unlike shareholders in a corporation, LLCs are not taxed as a separate business entity. Instead, all profits and losses are "passed through" the business to each member of the LLC. LLC members report profits and losses on their personal federal tax returns, just like the owners of a partnership would.

https://www.sba.gov/content/limited-liability-company-llc

Cooperative

A cooperative is a business or organization owned by and operated for the benefit of those using its services. Profits and earnings generated by the cooperative are distributed among the members, also known as user-owners.

Typically, an elected board of directors and officers run the cooperative while regular members have voting power to control the direction of the cooperative. Members can become part of the cooperative by purchasing shares, though the amount of shares they hold does not affect the weight of their vote.

Cooperatives are common in the healthcare, retail, agriculture, art and restaurant industries.

https://www.sba.gov/content/cooperative

Corporation

Corporation (C Corporation)

A corporation (sometimes referred to as a C corporation) is an independent legal entity owned by shareholders. This means that the corporation itself, not the shareholders that own it, is held legally liable for the actions and debts the business incurs.

Corporations are more complex than other business structures because they tend to have costly administrative fees and complex tax and legal requirements. Because of these issues, corporations are generally suggested for established, larger companies with multiple employees.

For businesses in that position, corporations offer the ability to sell ownership shares in the business through stock offerings. "Going public" through an initial public offering (IPO) is a major selling point in attracting investment capital and high quality employees.

https://www.sba.gov/content/corporation

Those are the best links for you to decide which one will work for you. Your tax advisor would be your best resource and the one to ask.

Research these to decide which will work for you. I am a Sole Proprietor and that works fine for me. You may also wish to ask your accountant or tax person what you would need to do. Each state and country has different requirements.

Writing as a Retail Business

EXPENSES

As a legal business with a Federal ID number and a state tax number (Easy to get on the internet under www.gov.com), you will have certain expenses that you may not have thought of before:

 WIFI or Internet expense, hosting fees for websites and some blogs, computer expense (repairs and maintenance), program software (updated or new), phone usage (monthly expenses), courses you may register for and attend, webcams either presented by you or someone else, podcast expense, updating to iPads, cameras you may rent or purchase, audio equipment you may buy, etc. . . All of these are deductible as business expenses. There are probably more. Don't overlook any trips you take for research. Remember to keep track of your expenses. (If you are in doubt about any of this, please consult your tax advisor who is an expert in this field.)

Although sitting in Starbucks using Google Search really isn't a research trip to claim expenses. Sorry!

Writing as a Retail Business

EMPLOYEES OR SUB-CONTRACTORS

Yes, you do have them. If you have an <u>accountant or bookkeeper</u> to do your monthly books or yearly taxes, that is an employee because you pay them. You probably have a <u>graphic designer</u> (book covers or interior design?) and <u>an editor</u> or more than one depending on their function, and you pay for their services, too. You most probably have <u>beta readers</u>, or readers who are not family but who read your manuscripts and give you Honest Feedback, right? I usually gift my Beta Readers with DD Cards or Starbucks cards. Most Beta readers don't expect to get paid, but a thoughtful gesture is always nice. Some authors have <u>virtual assistants.</u>

You will add to the list as your business grows and you decide what you need to delegate so

Writing as a Retail Business

that you can get down to the real business of writing. Your time is valuable and only you can decide where you want to spend it. This might be a good place to think about what you want to do and what you don't want to do.

A BUSINESS PLAN OUTLINE

Every business needs some plan, and as an author, you need to think about where you want your business to be in a year, or two or five. How many books will you finish and publish? I have just started to do this, and it does make life easier. I have an overall *yearly plan* and have broken it down into an *accomplish-by-monthly plan*.

On a 3 x 5 card, I write the yearly plan which might include some financial goals. More importantly, it might include your projected production goals (how many books you want to publish during the year.) I write these goals down on a 3 x 5 card (a favorite tool on my desk) and on an individual card, I write MY INTENT to accomplish for the month. One month might read:

Writing as a Retail Business

1. TYL downloads new files into audio (Thinking Your Life)

2. TO YOUR HEALTH edited and republished to Amazon, KOBO, NOOK, and BOOKLOCKER.

3. TYH new cover

4. TYH start audio book

5. Finish chapters 7, 8, 9 for Stones and Clones

Make sure each card begins with I INTEND TO ACCOMPLISH THE FOLLOWING:

You can be as detailed or as 'loose' as you want. I find I do better with loose goals because they can and do change.

I have put together a business plan that you can download for free from my website: www.audacious-publisher.com

YOUR IMPRINT

"Imprint: verb, to impress or stamp (a mark or outline) on a surface or body" Dictionary.com.

How will you make your IMPRINT in the world of readers? How will they identify with you? How will they find you? Part of your imprint is the genre you write in.

Traditionally writers were advised to write in only one genre, but times and readers' tastes have changed. They are much more eclectic, and authors are writing in several different genres, even publishing under different names.

Nora Roberts also publishes under J.D.Robb and Steven King sometimes writes as Richard Bachman to name a few.

I publish in Visionary Non-Fiction under Sharon D. Anderson, Ph.D., and my Visionary Fiction under S.D. Anderson.

Writing as a Retail Business

Your Genre, your Personal Website, Blogs, Podcasts, Social Media; (Facebook, Twitter), is where you declare your Imprinting, where you tell the world what you are doing, and where to find you. I do go into this in some of my blogs which you can access through my website.

Writing as a Retail Business

YOUR INVENTORY

I touched on this earlier. One book: nine possibilities. Some of those may or may not apply here. For this purpose, let's use the following:

One Manuscript:

1. A Print book,

2. An E-Book,

3. An Audio Book,

4. A translation.

5. A serial

6. Magazine serial

(6 possibilities from one manuscript)

If you have written five (5) books and the rights belong to you, multiply that by the six possibilities listed above, you now have twenty (30) pieces of potential inventory. Multiply that out by the four main sites, Amazon, Kobo, and

Writing as a Retail Business

Nook, and you have eighty (120) pieces of inventory.

I currently have 54 books on Amazon (my dashboard) multiplied out gives me endless possibilities, and that multiplied by the 4 main sites (Amazon, Kobo, and Nook) makes countless pieces of inventory that it stalled my brain. I could have added the 13 Amazon countries but my calculator just died…

If you want to consider translating your books into different languages; the following are booming markets: Spanish, German and Mandarin.

S.D. Anderson PhD

Writing as a Retail Business

SCALABLE CAREER

From this, perhaps you can see the benefits of a Scalable Career. You only need to write each manuscript once, change it into one of the 6 possibilities and you have a Scalable Career.

No wonder they call this "THE LAPTOP LIFE"

Your laptop is portable (desktops are slowly becoming obsolete) and can go wherever you decide you want to live, vacation or write. Several months ago, I downloaded Windows 10 onto my desk-top. I really lived to regret it and took the console to my computer gurus to have it removed. They were very busy and told me the wait would be longer than their one day turnaround. I said I was fine with that as I had a laptop which was gifted to me and I could continue to write on that. During that week, I became hooked on THE LAPTOP LIFE. So much so that used my laptop exclusively and that desktop was passed on to a family member for his side-business.

Now I own a Lenovo all-in-one and it serves me well for my publishing business.

It is interesting to note that my business also travels with me. Some people use their iPads and iPhones for this purpose and perhaps I shall come around to that point eventually. Whatever device you use is your choice. Your scalable career can go anywhere in the world, just like your books.

Writing as a Retail Business

MARKETING

Most authors have a huge fear around marketing and granted, it's time consuming and does take you away from your writing (which you would rather be doing). Owning a store with merchandise or inventory, as a good business owner you know that the inventory or merchandise doesn't fly off the shelves into the hands of consumers, you have to advertise to get potential buyers into your store.

There are hundreds of sites and books on the internet to help you with your marketing. My advice to you is to research this, ask other authors and see what works for them. Perhaps you will start with a blog, try it for a few months and see how that works for you.

Writing as a Retail Business

BLOG

I highly recommend www.blogger.com for your blog. You can start with their free sites and develop from there. This is the perfect place to start if you haven't blogged before.

I spoke about this in the last section but here is more information for you. This is not as overwhelming as you may think. You are a writer. A Blog is your way to communicate with your readers (the people interested in you and your books). I use my GoDaddy website and their tools for my blog. www.capecodwritersstudio.com

There are many sites for blogs, now. Go online and check them out.

What to write on a blog? Anything you think your readers and potential readers would enjoy reading about.

Writing as a Retail Business

Keep them informed with your progress on that new book. Ask them to help you with a title. Some authors offer free advanced copies in exchange for reviews. Your BLOG is a key marketing tool.

Writing as a Retail Business

PODCASTS

Podcasts are another way to market your books. Originally, my podcasts were created on Audacity for the track (**Audacity** is a free download) http://www.audacity.com

Saved as an MP3 file and uploaded to **PodOMatic**, which is also a free site.

http://podomatic.com

Now I use Another site for the all-in-one podcast is www.anchor.com They offer you a free site and you can start your podcast right there and even ad music in the background.

For professional Podcasts, you may want to consider another more complicated route. Professional Podcasts are easy, you do need a bit more equipment than for a blog.

1.   A small microphone – available through Amazon.com. Price range is under $10.00 for

Writing as a Retail Business

an inexpensive one to an expensive one that is really high tech. Depending on your laptop or computer, they are easy to use and plug in easily.

Some laptops come already equipped with a microphone.

2. Audacity – a free program to record your voice. http://www.audacity.com this program is fairly easy and if you have a teenager nearby to give their advice and guide you through it, all the better. There is also a drop down menu where you are guided to save this podcast as a MP3 file. That is the file that your readers can download onto their devices and listen to.

3. Pod-O-Matic - Open an account with Pod-O-Matic (free). Here is where you post the audio version of your blog. This is not really complicated. There are other sites out there to

use for podcasts. You can search and find the one best suited for your work.

4. <u>Content</u> - From experience, I write my blog and record that with Audacity. Save it as your MP3 file, post that on Pod-O-Matic. Or you can post it on Anchor.com. .

Writing as a Retail Business

E-mail Lists .

Growing your e-mail list is another marketing tool and you can download information from http://www.aweber.com – or www.constantcontact.com a great way to get things started. There are so many possibilities; some of those links are listed at the end of this book.

Your e-mail list is probably the most important component to your marketing. Here is where you capture your customers and keep them. The more you grow your list, the more readers you will accumulate. These are your FANS. They are the ones who anxiously await your next book. You need to keep them engaged and interested and they will be your FANS for life. How do you do that?

By being GENUINE.

Writing as a Retail Business

Your FANS will like you, sing your praises and spread the word about your books. This is one of the components that make Face Book so popular.

How do you add fans to your list? There are literally thousands of books, programs and ideas about how to do this. I will share someone I trust and his programs are good because he is GENUINE. His name is Yaro Stark and here is his link:

https://www.entrepreneurs-journey.com/

Yaro gives away a ton of information. You might want to check his site out.

You grow your list each time you do a presentation. You ask people to sign up to receive your newsletter or whatever else you want to offer. At the end of your blog, ask the recipient to send it on to others if they feel it will be of interest. The more readers you have the more readers you can help. And isn't that the name of the game?

When you have accumulated a big list, bigger than you want to deal with, you might want to check out a mailing house or system.

www.aweber.com or www.constantcontact.com they offer excellent services for the beginner and for the more established accounts.

WEBSITES

You need a website because…… a website is your store front. Here is where you list your books – your inventory for sale.

Your books may be out there on KOBO or AMAZON and that's great, BUT, when someone wants to know about you and what you write, the first link you give them is the link to your website. That is where they really find out who you are and what you write.

Anyone can access your books on Amazon, but that is only half of your story, isn't it?

The beauty of your own website is each book that you have written can have its own personal story. You have the opportunity to tell the world that this book took you 5 years to write, etc.…

Writing as a Retail Business

Where and how do you accomplish this? For my first websites, I used Homestead, which at the time was connected to my crystal shop through Quick Books. My suggestion to you now is to check out the different sites.

Both of my websites are on www.GoDaddy.com I like working on their site because the templates are easy. They do have some limitations, but I can change templates to update the look and never lose my content. That works for me.

They offers inexpensive websites and hosting I have recently added a store to one of my sites and can post my books and my new on-line courses and sell them there. This constitutes another marketing segment that I can use.

For a website and some of my marketing, my costs are approximately $250.00 per year for domain name, website, and hosting. Some authors use other sites, you can do the research and find the best one for you and your "Store Front".

This site also hosts my blog which I post easily and send out as an e-mail campaign. They also offer the option to send the blog to social media sites.

SOCIAL MEDIA

According to current marketing strategies, social media is a must. This appears to be the best track to take when publicizing your book.

<u>Facebook</u> – Create a business page and promote your books here. It is really simple and easy to do and most authors have a Facebook business page.

<u>Twitter</u> – another media that have helped other books and authors go viral. Sorry, I cannot counsel you on this one as I have not been able to master this aspect of marketing.

<u>Goodreads</u> – You should have an Author's Page on Goodreads. Here is where you get your reviews. Easy to set up and run. Amazon can help you here. Whatever books you have on Kindle can be automatically be posted here.

Writing as a Retail Business

<u>Amazon Author's Page</u> – an absolute must have. I was amazed at how professional my book covers looked on my Amazon page.

ROYALTIES

Bet you never thought I would get to this very important part. We all want to get paid for our books, or at least most people do. That is really the bottom line for a business, (the profits), what's left over after all of the business expenses are paid.

Our Royalties are our income. Depending on how you have published your books, (Traditional of Self-Publish) the payments can be deposited in your business account or wherever you decide to put the money.

Traditional publishing payments are usually done quarterly. I am not an expert here, so please make allowances.

Because I self-publish on Amazon, my notification of payment is sent to me about mid-month. The actual payments are dropped into my account around the first of the month for the previous month. Another words, a payment I receive the beginning of November is payment for books sold the entire month of September

There is less than a month's delay while all of the payments from the global locations are tallied and sent to Amazon to be finalized, and the currencies changed into U.S. Dollars.

When I publish books for others, I recommend they open their own account on KDP and set up their own banking which allows them to get their royalties immediately into their own checking account.

A PLAN FOR EACH BOOK

As I was doing my own business plan (Angelic Communications) I wanted to take a good look at each of my books and check them out to analyze why they were sitting on the screen and not doing anything.

Using 3 x 5 cards again, I used one card per book and did a checklist for each one.

Here it is:

TITLE OF THE BOOK IN QUESTION:

TITLE CHANGE?

Does this book need a title change? If it is in print, you can do this by creating a second edition and going through the print process again. If you are publishing digitally, you only need to make those changes in your Microsoft Manuscript saving it as a second edition. If you publish through Amazon.com and their KDP program, you have a dashboard and can make those changes easily BUT I would wait until I had gone through the checklist before making any changes there or to any other site.

COVER

Do you think a new cover will enhance the book? If you made a title change, then you do need a new cover. Not sure? Do some research; check out covers in the same categories and see what is selling and what would easily adapt to your book text. This is like buying and wearing a new outfit.

Author's Note: The cover for this book was created by the author on canva.com a user friendly site. Here is their link: http://www.canva.com

PRICING

Use the same considerations as above. See where the other books in your category are

Writing as a Retail Business

retailing for. Any shop owner knows that price comparison is a necessary decision. That also implies that you don't have to follow the pack and get into a price war.

Writing as a Retail Business

CATEGORIES

Have you placed your book in the right categories? Sometimes a change here is all that is needed to boost sales.

KEY WORDS

Another listing to consider. Key words are important and keep your book up front for the search engines. Yes, we still use those.

CONTENT

Does the story or the content need to be re-edited? Many times after a book is published, the author thinks of changes ... we all do it!

AUDIO BOOK

Is this another format you might want to consider?

TRANSLATION

Can you see this book published in another language?

PUBLISHING E-BOOKS

Here is where you decide if you want to use a service for publishing your books or do it yourself. There are two services that I know of, probably more: Smashwords and Draft2Digital (D2D). As more and more self-publishers come into this Indie arena, these services will become extremely popular. I am currently using D2D and find them tremendously helpful and user friendly.

I picture this service much like my personal agent. I give them the book and they send it out to the different sites: Amazon KDP, Kobo, Nook, Scribed, Inktera, and Tolino. Yes, they do take a small percentage, but you have to make that decision, and that is only when the book sells.

I don't want to think of the time it would take me to do all of this individually. Also, just to

Writing as a Retail Business

keep track of this is a nightmare. When would I write?

Writing as a Retail Business

PRINTED EDITION

This is your decision. If you have a book in your inventory and want to create a print edition, that is up to you. I would recommend Cape Cod Publishing, which is a P.O.D. Service. (Print on Demand).

SERIES

If you have written several books in a series, then you might want to consider publishing them as a 'bundle' or offer the first one in the series free so that the rest will automatically be purchased by the reader.

FREE SITES

I will list a few sites you can tap into to offer your book for free: Freebooksy.com BookGorilla.com, and Booksends.com There are hundreds more, I am certain, all that is needed is to Google them… I have used

Writing as a Retail Business

Amazon's KDP promotional offers and had a lot of my books downloaded globally. That was fun to watch...

MARKETING STRATEGIES

This area is very important. Writing and Publishing are only half of the story. Here are some of the key ingredients you really should have.

1. Website (storefront)

2. Blog

3. Podcasts

4. Social Media

5. Facebook

6. Amazon's Author's page

7. Twitter

8. Goodread's

9. Instagram

10. YouTube

11. Pinterest

And more that you will probably find on-line.

Writing as a Retail Business

Some Built-in Marketing Strategies

THE HOOK

What is THE HOOK?

The HOOK is what you use to HOOK your readers, to HOOK their attention, to hopefully get them interested enough to buy your book. It is your one and only chance to "Make the Sale or Get the Job." If that sounds unusual, it isn't really, it's salesmanship.

Let's try this.

You have written a book. You want to publish it because:

1. You think it is good.
2. You want to share it with others.
3. You want people to buy it.
4. You want to make money.

Writing as a Retail Business

5. You want to get paid for your work.
6. You want to help people.
7. You want to inspire people.
8. You want to entertain people.
9. You want to educate people.
10. You love to write and you could care less if people buy your book.

(Perhaps we should leave that one out?)

You do have several chances to make that first impression, not unlike meeting someone for the first time. It's like a job interview, and in a way, that is exactly what is happening. Someone is interviewing you, (a potential reader), and you hope they will buy your book. (You will get the job)
The first thing they see is your TITLE.

HOOK #1 – TITLE

Writing as a Retail Business

On Amazon or any book site, the TITLE is your first HOOK. If the Title holds no appeal to the reader, he/she will slide right by yours until he/she finds one that will catch their interest. (These are all Marketing Strategies, by the way.)

The MODERN READER or TODAYS READER is usually on their mobile device, computer, IPhone, and surfing to find something of interest. Unless they specifically know what it is they are looking for, they are surfing. They are already in their chosen category (Fiction, Non-fiction, Romance. Action/Adventure, etc.) That part is already accomplished.

What does your title say about your book? Does it reflect some sense of the book? Are you completely satisfied with this title? One of the benefits of Self-Publishing, especially on Amazon and KDP (Kindle Direct Publishing), is, you do have the option to make changes. Choose your title carefully so that it reflects what your book is about. If there is something about the title you aren't comfortable with, then work on making it better. Remember, this is what will attract your reader.

HOOK #2 COVER

Your potential reader likes your title, it's interesting and is a possibility. The next thing your reader looks at is your COVER. Covers that are terribly busy and have lots of action, illustrations, printing, do have merits, remember, the reader is going to be looking at a THUMBNAIL, a postage stamp size of your cover, so plan accordingly. <u>Sometimes less is better</u>. The key ingredients here are <u>book title, sub-title (if one) and Author's name</u>. These are what MUST show in the thumbnail of your cover.

There are numerous possibilities for you to consider for your cover. KDP and CreateSpace

Writing as a Retail Business

do offer Cover Creator, a program, with which you can DIY a decent cover. I have used both programs and had good results. You can also employ the services of a graphic artist who will create the whole thing for you, also which I have done for some of my books. Todd Engel has designed many of my covers. Here is his information at

https://www.facebook.com/Todd-Engel-Engel-Creative-Graphic-Design/

You will see one of my book covers right in the middle of his banner-display. (Angels in Action) A web based program (free) for graphic design is Canva.com.

Here is their link:https://www.canva.com This program is free to use, and they do offer royalty free graphics. You can also purchase graphics for a very nominal fee.

HOOK # 3 YOUR BLURB.

Your BLURB is your introduction or the short paragraph that you will use for the back of your book cover or the paragraph that you will use to best describe what your book is about when you enter this information into the KDP program. This information will be what the public will read when they look at your landing page (the basic page on Amazon that has your cover thumbnail, price, and other pertinent information). KDP has already set up this page for you, free, and this is where your potential reader will be automatically forwarded to when they click on the thumbnail of your cover.

This HOOK #3, Your Blurb, should answer these questions:

WHO

WHAT

Writing as a Retail Business

WHERE

WHEN

WHY

HOW

This blurb will be like a news story on the front page of a newspaper. It should answer those questions, in fact, that is where those W's came from (journalism).

To break that list down, let's do this:

1. WHO – the who is your main character- who are you writing this book about?
2. WHAT – is happening to this character that the reader should, or might want to identify with, to know more about (the plot)
3. WHERE – where is this taking place? in Chicago, Illinois, along the

Writing as a Retail Business

Amazon River, the Angelic Kingdom? The reader should have some point of reference.

4. WHEN – when is this happening? Years ago, right now, in the future?
5. WHY – what cataclysmic event has happened to the protagonist (hero/heroine) that you have written a story about? Why should the reader read on?
6. HOW - will it be resolved? How will this story end? Make this point like a cliff hanger to make the reader WANT to buy the book. (The Sale, or The Job.)

HOOK #4 FIRST CHAPTER

Amazon KDP offers potential readers a peek (look inside) at the first few chapters of your book, right on your landing page, which gives the reader a better idea of what your book is all about. This is a clever bit of marketing that KDP has already done for you. Your first chapter should also answer those five 'W' questions. Here is where you set up your story (plot) and characters. If they get this far, they are interested, and will probably purchase the book, if not now, then soon. KDP also offers the following, (built right into your landing page)

Read for free – Kindle Unlimited – you still get royalties for this option.

Kindle Matchbook – which ties your print and e-book together.

Buy now with one click – making this easy for the reader.

Deliver to the reader's device (iPhone, tablet, etc.)

Send a free sample

Writing as a Retail Business

Give as a gift

Add to your list (this has a pull-down screen with the following:

Kindle Wish List (private)

Shopping list

Kindle Wish List (public)

Gift Ideas List

And finally, if none of the above work, *a Create a List option*.

So, you see, Amazon has done all this marketing for you, and obviously offers all these choices so the reader does not leave your landing page empty-handed. All very clever marketing tools, which benefits both the Author and Amazon.

HOOK # 5 – YOUR BIO

Writing as a Retail Business

Authors Bio and photo – readers want to know who wrote the book and sometimes why they wrote it. Your bio can be short but do give the reader a brief look into your life.

NOW, TO SUMMARIZE:

Your FIVE Hooks:

TITLE, COVER, BLURB, FIRST CHAPTER AND AUTHOR'S BIO

REMEMBER:

IF THEY DON'T GET THE HOOK,

THEY WON'T BUY THE BOOK

More on Advertising - Marketing

Several more sites that you should consider for your advertising. (marketing)

These are sites I use and I consider them worthy of your notice. Even if you chose not to use them, they deserve an honorable mention.

Written Word Media

This is a newer site and has not raised their prices for several years.(novelty)

They offer four separate categories to market in: Freebooksy, Bargainbooksy, Red Feather Romance and Book Stacks.

The premise is you rent their site and their e-mail list for a day and your book is displayed for purchase. I have had excellent luck with this site. I used Bargain Booksy for several of my novels and they did well.

Writing as a Retail Business

I find their prices reasonable and they offer a large list of genres for you to choose from. You can also be on their subscription list to see what they are offering. I use this site for two purposes, to research what is being offered and to read some of the books. Ideal combination.

This is digital marketing.(e-books only)

Here is their link:

https://www.writtenwordmedia.com

Draft2Digital or D2D

Next is D2D or Draft2Digital which is another site I use and recommend.

D2D is a different format. You don't advertise with them. Instead, you post your e-book to their site and they send it out to 10 or 11 different sites. They do charge a fee of 10% but I consider that an agent's fee because if I had to cover all of these sites I would have no time to write.

Here are a few of their sites:

BARNES&NOBLE
BOOKSELLERS

OverDrive

Rakuten kobo

ⅢⅠ bibliotheca

24symbols

RESOURCES

all in one place

Publishers P.O.D.

http://www.booklocker.com

Inspiration and Information

http://www.thecreativepenn.com

Publishing Services for E-Books

https://www.writtenwordmedia.com

http://www.smashwords.com

http://www.draft2digitaal.com

http://www.scribed.com

http://www.inktera.com

http://www.tolino.com

http://www.fiverr.com

Writing as a Retail Business

Free Book Sites:

http://www.bookbub.com

http://www.freebooksy.com

http://www.bookgorilla.com

http://www.booksends.com

Author Stats

http://www.authorearningsreport.com

Small Business Administration

http://www.sba.gov.com

http://www.gov.com

Blogs, websites, podcasts, e-mails

http://www.wordpress.com

http://www.blogger.com

S.D. Anderson PhD

Writing as a Retail Business

http://www.audacity.com

http://www.podomatic.com

http://www.aweber.com

https://constantcontact.com

Book Covers

http://www.canva.com

My sites:

http://www.audacious-author.com

https://www.audacious-publisher.com

https://www.capecodwritersstudio.com

S.D. Anderson PhD

Writing as a Retail Business

I sincerely hope this guide will be helpful for your writing career (whatever you decide to do). With this guide my only intent is to "plant seeds and ideas". It is up to you to water and fertilize them.

Happy Writing

Sharon

THANK YOU

Thank you for choosing this print and e-book. I hope you've found the information interesting.

If you loved this book, found it useful, and have a moment to spare, **I would really appreciate a short review on the site where you purchased. Your help in spreading the word is gratefully received!**

Writing as a Retail Business

Also by S. D. Anderson

Available As E-Book Format

Available In Print ** Starred

Visionary Fiction

Atlantis – The Final Days**

Angels in Action

A Cape Cod Romance

Stones and Bones**

A Christmas Wish**

Dear Angels**

Cape Cod Cozy Mysteries

Potts Better Butter Bakery (2020)

The Something Series

Something Witchy the pilot**

Writing as a Retail Business

Something Witchy – Book one**

Something Sinister - Book two**

Something Bloody - Book three**

Something Loverly - Book four**

Something Merry – Book five**

Something Weird – Book six -2021

<u>Visionary Non-Fiction</u>

Creating Crystal Grids**

Sacred Grids**

Crystal Grids for Light Bodies

Crystal Grids for Personal Protection**

What Are You Thinking? **

Cosmic Blueprint**

Raising Your Energy**

Body Blogs for Health**

Writing as a Retail Business

Children's Book

Tuk-Tuk the Rabbit**

The Black Shadow**

Spiritual Guidelines Series

Now a Boxed Set*

Prosperity Workbook

Remarkable Relationships

To Your Health**

Everyone is Evolving

ON WRITING

Writing as a Retail Business**

Creating a Paperback in KDP**

Blueprinting for Successful Self-Publishing**

The Blue Book of Self-Publishing**

S.D. Anderson PhD

Writing as a Retail Business

Writing as a Retail Business

Sharon D. Anderson, PhD, RMT

Sharon is an Author/Publisher, dedicated to her craft for more years than she wishes to acknowledge. She writes Heavenly Cozy Mysteries, and other visionary stuff which reflect her wisdom, insights, and a lot of silly humor.

She is the Founder of the Cape Cod Writers' Studios, which meet weekly in Dennisport, Centerville, and Cotuit where she teaches members the intricacies of professional self-publishing, plying them with lots of cups of tea when they are overwhelmed.

She also has memberships in Visionary Fiction Alliance, and the Cape Cod Media Center,

Writing as a Retail Business

E-mail: sdanderson.books@gmail.com

Her Blog:
https://www.capecodwritersstudio.com

Her website: https://www.audacious-publisher.com

NOTES

Writing as a Retail Business

NOTES

Writing as a Retail Business

NOTES

Writing as a Retail Business

www.ingramcontent.com/pod-product-compliance
Lightning Source LLC
Chambersburg PA
CBHW050008230526
45465CB00003BB/1312